EDWARD LEAR'S
GROMBOOLIAN
POEMS

She has gone to the great Gromboolian plain,
And we probably never shall meet again!

The Pelican Chorus

EDWARD LEAR'S
GROMBOOLIAN POEMS

Illustrated by Jenny Thorne

MACMILLAN CHILDREN'S BOOKS

FOREWORD

An interest in the poems of Edward Lear has led me to speculate on the appearance of 'the land where the Bong-tree grows' (to which the Owl and the Pussy-Cat sailed). There is little doubt that Mr Lear was referring to the Great Gromboolian Plain, the Hills of the Chankly Bore and the Coromandel Coast, and the publishers of the present work have kindly invited me to provide illustrations of the region.

In the pages which follow I have included topographical views and depictions of the flora and fauna as a complement to some of Mr Lear's best-known poems. Brief explanatory notes on details in the pictures have been given where they would seem to be useful.

Jenny Thorne

Illustrations © 1983 Jenny Thorne

Edward Lear's A Book of Nonsense was first published in 1846.

This edition of seven of his best-known poems first published 1983 by
MACMILLAN CHILDREN'S BOOKS
A division of Macmillan Publishers Limited
London and Basingstoke
Associated companies throughout the world

Picturemac edition published 1987

British Library Cataloguing in Publication Data
Lear, Edward
Edward Lear's Gromboolian poems.
I. Title   II. Thorne, Jenny
821'.8   PR4879.L2

ISBN 0-333-43925-2

Printed in Hong Kong

CONTENTS

Flora

THE JUMBLIES

THEY went to sea in a Sieve, they did,
    In a Sieve they went to sea:
    In spite of all their friends could say,
On a winter's morn, on a stormy day,
    In a Sieve they went to sea!
And when the Sieve turned round and round,
And every one cried, "You'll all be drowned!"
They called aloud, "Our Sieve ain't big,
"But we don't care a button! we don't care a fig!
    "In a Sieve we'll go to sea!"
        Far and few, far and few,
            Are the lands where the Jumblies live;
            Their heads are green, and their hands are blue,
            And they went to sea in a Sieve.

They sailed away in a Sieve, they did,
    In a Sieve they sailed so fast,
With only a beautiful pea-green veil
Tied with a riband by way of a sail,
    To a small tobacco-pipe mast;
And every one said, who saw them go,
"O won't they be soon upset you know!
"For the sky is dark, and the voyage is long,
"And happen what may, it's extremely wrong
    "In a Sieve to sail so fast!"
        Far and few, far and few,
            Are the lands where the Jumblies live;
            Their heads are green, and their hands are blue,
            And they went to sea in a Sieve.

The water it soon came in, it did,
    The water it soon came in;
So to keep them dry, they wrapped their feet
In a pinky paper all folded neat,
    And they fastened it down with a pin.
And they passed the night in a crockery-jar,
And each of them said, "How wise we are!
"Though the sky be dark, and the voyage be long,
"Yet we never can think we were rash or wrong,
    "While round in our Sieve we spin!"
        Far and few, far and few,
            Are the lands where the Jumblies live;
            Their heads are green, and their hands are blue,
            And they went to sea in a Sieve.

1. Washtubbia Circularis

2. Plumbunnia Nutritiosa N.B. The
   flower is white

3. Cockatooca Superba

4. Tigerlillia Terribilis

5. Smalltoothcombia Domestica

The Hills of the Chankly Bore

And all night long they sailed away;
    And when the sun went down,
They whistled and warbled a moony song
To the echoing sound of a coppery gong,
    In the shade of the mountains brown.
"O Timballo! How happy we are,
"When we live in a sieve and a crockery-jar.
"And all night long in the moonlight pale,
"We sail away with a pea-green sail,
    "In the shade of the mountains brown!"
        Far and few, far and few,
            Are the lands where the Jumblies live;
            Their heads are green, and their hands are blue.
            And they went to sea in a Sieve.

They sailed to the Western Sea, they did,
    To a land all covered with trees,
And they bought an Owl, and a useful Cart,
And a pound of Rice, and a Cranberry Tart,
    And a hive of silvery Bees.
And they bought a Pig, and some green Jackdaws,
And a lovely Monkey with lollipop paws,
And forty bottles of Ring-Bo-Ree,
    And no end of Stilton Cheese.
        Far and few, far and few,
            Are the lands where the Jumblies live;
            Their heads are green, and their hands are blue,
            And they went to sea in a Sieve.

And in twenty years they all came back,
    In twenty years or more,
And every one said, "How tall they've grown!
"For they've been to the Lakes, and the Terrible Zone,
    "And the Hills of the Chankly Bore;"
And they drank their health, and gave them a feast
Of dumplings made of beautiful yeast;
And every one said, "If we only live,
"We too will go to sea in a Sieve, –
    "To the Hills of the Chankly Bore!"
        Far and few, far and few,
            Are the lands where the Jumblies live;
            Their heads are green, and their hands are blue,
            And they went to sea in a Sieve.

1. Ape Indigo

2. Guittara Pensilis

3. Jackdora Peaculiaris. *A ravenous bird which nests near brooks, is constantly crowing and has magpie tendencies*

4. Cranberri Veritartus

The Gromboolian Plain by night

THE DONG
WITH A LUMINOUS NOSE

WHEN awful darkness and silence reign
  Over the great Gromboolian plain,
 Through the long, long wintry nights;–
When the angry breakers roar
As they beat on the rocky shore;–
 When Storm-clouds brood on the towering heights
Of the Hills of the Chankly Bore:–

Then, through the vast and gloomy dark,
There moves what seems a fiery spark,
 A lonely spark with silvery rays
 Piercing the coal-black night, –
 A meteor strange and bright:–
Hither and thither the vision strays,
 A single lurid light.

Slowly it wanders, – pauses, – creeps, –
Anon it sparkles, – flashes and leaps;
And ever as onward it gleaming goes
A light on the Bong-tree stems it throws.
And those who watch at that midnight hour
From Hall or Terrace, or lofty Tower,
Cry, as the wild light passes along, –
  "The Dong! – the Dong!
 "The wandering Dong through the forest goes!
  "The Dong! – the Dong!
  "The Dong with a luminous Nose!"

1. Mistmia Gaino *The Gromboolian
  Snipe flies in zig-zags and is not easily
  avoided*

2. Tickia Orologica. *Wild Time,
  commonly infested with ticks*

3. Batsinthe Belfrii

4. Chimpunki Wooliae

Long years ago
The Dong was happy and gay,
Till he fell in love with a Jumbly Girl
Who came to those shores one day.
For the Jumblies came in a Sieve, they did, –
Landing at eve near the Zemmery Fidd
Where the Oblong Oysters grow,
And the rocks are smooth and gray.
And all the woods and the valleys rang
With the Chorus they daily and nightly sang, –
"Far and few, far and few,
Are the lands where the Jumblies live;
Their heads are green, and their hands are blue,
And they went to sea in a Sieve."

Happily, happily passed those days!
While the cheerful Jumblies staid;
They danced in circlets all night long,
To the plaintive pipe of the lively Dong,
In moonlight, shine, or shade.
For day and night he was always there
By the side of the Jumbly Girl so fair,
With her sky-blue hands, and her sea-green hair,
Till the morning came of that hateful day
When the Jumblies sailed in their Sieve away,
And the Dong was left on the cruel shore
Gazing – gazing for evermore, –
Ever keeping his weary eyes on
That pea-green sail on the far horizon, –
Singing the Jumbly Chorus still
As he sate all day on the grassy hill, –
"Far and few, far and few,
Are the lands where the Jumblies live;
Their heads are green, and their hands are blue,
And they went to sea in a Sieve."

But when the sun was low in the West,
The Dong arose and said, –
"What little sense I once possessed
"Has quite gone out of my head!"

1. Crumpetti Giganticum. *Said to be the largest species of water lily*

2. Twangum Dogwoodiae. *Noted for its bark*

3. Bongus Grombooliensis. *The celebrated and beautiful Bong tree*

Some native trees

And since that day he wanders still
By lake and forest, marsh and hill,
Singing – "O somewhere, in valley or plain
"Might I find my Jumbly Girl again!
"For ever I'll seek by lake and shore
"Till I find my Jumbly Girl once more!"

Playing a pipe with silvery squeaks,
Since then his Jumbly Girl he seeks,
And because by night he could not see,
He gathered the bark of the Twangum Tree
On the flowery plain that grows.
And he wove him a wondrous Nose, –
A nose as strange as a Nose could be!
Of vast proportions and painted red,
And tied with cords to the back of his head.
– In a hollow rounded space it ended
With a luminous lamp within suspended
All fenced about
With a bandage stout
To prevent the wind from blowing it out; –
And with holes all round to send the light,
In gleaming rays on the dismal night.

And now each night, and all night long,
Over those plains still roams the Dong;
And above the wail of the Chimp and Snipe
You may hear the squeak of his plaintive pipe
While ever he seeks, but seeks in vain
To meet with his Jumbly Girl again;
Lonely and wild – all night he goes, –
The Dong with a luminous Nose!
And all who watch at the midnight hour,
From Hall or Terrace, or lofty Tower,
Cry, as they trace the Meteor bright,
Moving along through the dreary night, –
"This is the hour when forth he goes,
"The Dong with a luminous Nose!
"Yonder – over the plain he goes;
"He goes!
"He goes;
"The Dong with a luminious Nose!"

1. Cranium Vacantis. *Eats frogs*

2. Leapupstiltus Dubious. *Eats frogs*

3. Quackia Eiderdowniensis. *Eats frogs*

4. Hopihae measelitis. *An endangered species, eats shrimps*

5. Flimpijimpi Shrimpi. *Eats watercress*

6. Nastitueetum aquamarina. *Watercress*

The Lakes

Woodland Life

THE OWL
AND THE PUSSY-CAT

THE Owl and the Pussy-Cat went to sea
    In a beautiful pea-green boat,
     They took some honey, and plenty of money,
  Wrapped up in a five-pound note.
The Owl looked up to the stars above,
    And sang to a small guitar,
"O lovely Pussy! O Pussy, my love,
    "What a beautiful Pussy you are,
       "You are,
       "You are!
  "What a beautiful Pussy you are!"

Pussy said to the Owl, "You elegant fowl!
    "How charmingly sweet you sing!
"O let us be married! too long we have tarried:
    "But what shall we do for a ring?"
They sailed away for a year and a day,
    To the land where the Bong-tree grows,
And there in a wood a Piggy-wig stood,
    With a ring at the end of his nose,
       His nose,
       His nose,
  With a ring at the end of his nose.

"Dear Pig, are you willing to sell for one shilling
    "Your ring?" Said the Piggy, "I will."
So they took it away, and were married next day
    By the Turkey who lives on the hill.
They dinèd on mince, and slices of quince,
    Which they ate with a runcible spoon;
And hand in hand, on the edge of the sand,
    They danced by the light of the moon,
       The moon,
       The moon,
  They danced by the light of the moon.

1. Verituf Exmasdinna

2. Plumbunnia Nutritiosa

3. Bacons Andwichis

The Coast of Coromandel

THE COURTSHIP OF
THE YONGHY-BONGHY-BÒ

ON the Coast of Coromandel
 Where the early pumpkins blow,
 In the middle of the woods
 Lived the Yonghy-Bonghy-Bò.
Two old chairs, and half a candle, –
One old jug without a handle, –
 These were all his worldly goods:
 In the middle of the woods,
 These were all the worldly goods,
 Of the Yonghy-Bonghy-Bò,
 Of the Yonghy-Bonghy-Bò.

Once, among the Bong-trees walking
 Where the early pumpkins blow,
 To a little heap of stones
 Came the Yonghy-Bonghy-Bò.
There he heard a Lady talking,
To some milk-white Hens of Dorking, –
 " 'Tis the Lady Jingly Jones!
 "On that little heap of stones
 "Sits the Lady Jingly Jones!"
 Said the Yonghy-Bonghy-Bò.
 Said the Yonghy-Bonghy-Bò.

"Lady Jingly! Lady Jingly!
 "Sitting where the pumpkins blow,
 "Will you come and be my wife?"
 Said the Yonghy-Bonghy-Bò.
"I am tired of living singly, –
"On this coast so wild and shingly, –
 "I'm a-weary of my life;
 "If you'll come and be my wife,
 "Quite serene would be my life!" –
 Said the Yonghy-Bonghy-Bò,
 Said the Yonghy-Bonghy-Bò.

"On this Coast of Coromandel,
 "Shrimps and watercresses grow,
 "Prawns are plentiful and cheap,"
 Said the Yonghy-Bonghy-Bò.

1. Squashia Antiquitas

2. Chickabidi Albiones. *An introduced species*

3. Quince Extreemlitartus

"You shall have my chairs and candle,
"And my jug without a handle! –
        "Gaze upon the rolling deep
        ("Fish is plentiful and cheap);
        "As the sea, my love is deep!"
    Said the Yonghy-Bonghy-Bò,
    Said the Yonghy-Bonghy-Bò.

Lady Jingly answered sadly,
    And her tears began to flow, –
        "Your proposal comes too late,
    "Mr. Yonghy-Bonghy-Bò!
"I would be your wife most gladly!"
(Here she twirled her fingers madly)
        "But in England I've a mate!
        "Yes! you've asked me far too late,
        "For in England I've a mate,
    "Mr. Yonghy-Bonghy-Bò!
    "Mr. Yonghy-Bonghy-Bò!

"Mr. Jones – (his name is Handel, –
    "Handel Jones, Esquire, & Co.)
        "Dorking fowls delights to send,
    "Mr. Yonghy-Bonghy-Bò!
"Keep, oh! keep your chairs and candle,
"And your jug without a handle, –
        "I can merely be your friend!
        "– Should my Jones more Dorkings send,
        "I will give you three, my friend!
    "Mr. Yonghy-Bonghy-Bò!
    "Mr. Yonghy-Bonghy-Bò!

"Though you've such a tiny body,
    "And your head so large doth grow, –
        "Though your hat may blow away,
    "Mr. Yonghy-Bonghy-Bò!
"Though you're such a Hoddy Doddy –
"Yet I wish that I could modi-
        "fy the words I needs must say!
        "Will you please to go away?
        "That is all I have to say –
    "Mr. Yonghy-Bonghy-Bò!"
    "Mr. Yonghy-Bonghy-Bò!"

The Bay of Gurtle

Down the slippery slopes of Myrtle,
   Where the early pumpkins blow,
      To the calm and silent sea
   Fled the Yonghy-Bonghy-Bò.
There, beyond the Bay of Gurtle,
Lay a large and lively Turtle; –
      "You're the Cove," he said, "for me;
      "On your back beyond the sea,
      "Turtle, you shall carry me!"
Said the Yonghy-Bonghy-Bò,
Said the Yonghy-Bonghy-Bò.

Through the silent-roaring ocean
   Did the Turtle swiftly go;
      Holding fast upon his shell
   Rode the Yonghy-Bonghy-Bò.
With a sad primæval motion
Towards the sunset isles of Boshen
      Still the Turtle bore him well.
      Holding fast upon his shell,
      "Lady Jingly Jones, farewell!"
Sang the Yonghy-Bonghy-Bò,
Sang the Yonghy-Bonghy-Bò.

From the Coast of Coromandel,
   Did that Lady never go;
      On that heap of stones she mourns
   For the Yonghy-Bonghy-Bò.
On that Coast of Coromandel,
In his jug without a handle,
      Still she weeps, and daily moans;
      On that little heap of stones
      To her Dorking Hens she moans,
For the Yonghy-Bonghy-Bò,
For the Yonghy-Bonghy-Bò.

1. Tortoisa Ultramarina

2. Scampi Scamperando

3. Mollusca Oblonga. *The oblong oyster produces a unique square pearl*

Shore life

The Western Sea and the Isles of Boshen

THE DADDY LONG-LEGS
AND THE FLY

ONCE Mr. Daddy Long-Legs,
   Dressed in brown and gray,
   Walked about upon the sands
   Upon a summer's day;
And there among the pebbles,
   When the wind was rather cold,
He met with Mr. Floppy Fly,
   All dressed in blue and gold.
And as it was too soon to dine,
They drank some Periwinkle-wine,
And played an hour two, or more,
At battlecock and shuttledore.

Said Mr. Daddy Long-Legs
   To Mr. Floppy Fly,
"Why do you never come to court?
   "I wish you'd tell me why.
"All gold and shine, in dress so fine,
   "You'd quite delight the court.
"Why do you never go at all?
   "I really think you *ought!*
"And if you went, you'd see such sights!
"Such rugs! and jugs! and candle-lights!
"And more than all, the King and Queen,
"One in red, and one in green!"

"O Mr. Daddy Long-Legs,"
   Said Mr. Floppy Fly,
"It's true I never go to court,
   "And I will tell you why.
"If I had six long legs like yours,
   "At once I'd go to court!
"But oh! I can't, because *my* legs
   "Are so extremely short.
"And I'm afraid the King and Queen
"(One in red, and one in green)
"Would say aloud, 'You are not fit,
"'You Fly, to come to court a bit!'"

"O Mr. Daddy Long-Legs,"
   Said Mr. Floppy Fly,
"I wish you'd sing one little song!
   "One mumbian melody!

The Western Sea lies to the east of the Gromboolian plain. It is so named as a politeness to visitors. On June 21 of each year it is the scene of the celebrated Boshen sailing race.

"You used to sing so awful well
    "In former days gone by,
"But now you never sing at all;
    "I wish you'd tell me why:
"For if you would, the silvery sound
"Would please the shrimps and cockles round,
"And all the crabs would gladly come
"To hear you sing, 'Ah, Hum di Hum!'"
Said Mr. Daddy Long-Legs,
    "I can never sing again!
"And if you wish, I'll tell you why,
    "Although it gives me pain.
"For years I could not hum a bit,
    "Or sing the smallest song;
"And this the dreadful reason is,
    "My legs are grown too long!
"My six long legs, all here and there,
"Oppress my bosom with despair;
"And if I stand, or lie, or sit,
"I cannot sing one single bit!"

So Mr. Daddy Long-Legs
    And Mr. Floppy Fly
Sat down in silence by the sea,
    And gazed upon the sky.
They said, "This is a dreadful thing!
    "The world has all gone wrong,
"Since one has legs too short by half,
    "The other much too long!
"One never more can go to court,
"Because his legs have grown too short;
"The other cannot sing a song,
"Because his legs have grown too long!"

Then Mr. Daddy Long-Legs
    And Mr. Floppy Fly
Rushed downward to the foaming sea
    With one sponge-taneous cry;
And there they found a little boat
    Whose sails were pink and gray;
And off they sailed among the waves
    Far, and far away.
They sailed across the silent main
And reached the great Gromboolian plain;
And there they play for evermore
At battlecock and shuttledore.*

1. Furrimbombus Buzziflora

2. Hunnibee Droniensis

3. Paterflae Clatterpedes

4. Flopiflae Dirtitosis

5. Caravanis Cranberrio. *The Coromandel snail lives exclusively on cranberry leaves. It is often mistaken for a cranberry and vice versa*

6. Cranberri Veritartus

7. Pollybirdia Singularis

   *Battlecock and Shuttledore: *a type of aerial curling*

26

Insects of the Gromboolian Plain

THE
QUANGLE WANGLE'S
HAT

ON the top of the Crumpetty Tree
    The Quangle Wangle sat,
But his face you could not see,
    On account of his Beaver Hat.
For his Hat was a hundred and two feet wide,
With ribbons and bibbons on every side
And bells, and buttons, and loops, and lace,
So that nobody ever could see the face
        Of the Quangle Wangle Quee.

The Quangle Wangle said
    To himself on the Crumpetty Tree, –
"Jam; and jelly; and bread;
    "Are the best of food for me!
"But the longer I live on this Crumpetty Tree,
"The plainer than ever it seems to me
"That very few people come this way,
"And that life on the whole is far from gay!"
        Said the Quangle Wangle Quee.

1. Ape Indigo

2. Ursaminor Olympicus

3. Tutancowmun Orientalis. *An introduced species*

28

Some animals of the Gromboolian Plain

But there came to the Crumpetty Tree,
    Mr. and Mrs. Canary;
And they said, – "Did ever you see
    "Any spot so charmingly airy?
"May we build a nest on your lovely Hat?
"Mr. Quangle Wangle, grant us that!
"O please let us come and build a nest
"Of whatever material suits you best,
        "Mr. Quangle Wangle Quee!"

And besides, to the Crumpetty Tree
    Came the Stork, the Duck, and the Owl;
The Snail and the Bumble-Bee,
    The Frog and the Fimble Fowl;
(The Fimble Fowl, with a Corkscrew leg);
And all of them said, – "We humbly beg,
"We may build our homes on your lovely Hat, –
"Mr. Quangle Wangle, grant us that!
        "Mr. Quangle Wangle Quee!"

And the Golden Grouse came there,
    And the Pobble who has no toes, –
And the small Olympian bear, –
    And the Dong with a luminous Nose.
And the Blue Baboon, who played the flute, –
And the Orient Calf from the Land of Tute, –
And the Attery Squash, and the Bisky Bat, –
All came and built on the lovely Hat
        Of the Quangle Wangle Quee.

And the Quangle Wangle said
    To himself on the Crumpetty Tree, –
"When all these creatures move
    "What a wonderful noise there'll be!"
And at night by the light of the Mulberry moon
They danced to the Flute of the Blue Baboon,
On the broad green leaves of the Crumpetty Tree,
And all were as happy as happy could be,
        With the Quangle Wangle Quee.

1. Grumblior Goldenae

2. Poppicockia Flexipedes

3. Pritiburdus Buttercuppia

4. Hoota Nocturno

Native birds

HOW PLEASANT TO KNOW MR. LEAR!

"How pleasant to know Mr. Lear!"
    Who has written such volumes of stuff!
Some think him ill-tempered and queer,
    But a few think him pleasant enough.

His mind is concrete and fastidious,
    His nose is remarkably big;
His visage is more or less hideous,
    His beard it resembles a wig.

He has ears, and two eyes, and ten fingers,
    Leastways if you reckon two thumbs;
Long ago he was one of the singers,
    But now he is one of the dumbs.

He sits in a beautiful parlour,
    With hundreds of books on the wall;
He drinks a great deal of Marsala,
    But never gets tipsy at all.

He has many friends, laymen and clerical,
    Old Foss is the name of his cat:
His body is perfectly spherical,
    He weareth a runcible hat.

When he walks in a waterproof white,
    The children run after him so!
Calling out, "He's come out in his night-
    grown, that crazy old Englishman, oh!"

He weeps by the side of the ocean,
    He weeps on the top of the hill;
He purchases pancakes and lotion,
    And chocolate shrimps from the mill.

He reads but he cannot speak Spanish,
    He cannot abide ginger-beer:
Ere the days of his pilgrimage vanish,
    How pleasant to know Mr. Lear!